COUNCIL *on*
FOREIGN
RELATIONS

Annual Report

2019

Annual Report
July 1, 2018–June 30, 2019

Council on Foreign Relations

58 East 68th Street
New York, NY 10065
tel 212.434.9400

1777 F Street, NW
Washington, DC 20006
tel 202.509.8400

cfr.org
communications@cfr.org

Contents

Mission Statement

The Council on Foreign Relations (CFR) is an independent, nonpartisan membership organization, think tank, and publisher dedicated to being a resource for its members, government officials, business executives, journalists, educators and students, civic and religious leaders, and other interested citizens in order to help them better understand the world and the foreign policy choices facing the United States and other countries.

Founded in 1921, CFR takes no institutional positions on matters of policy. CFR carries out its mission by

- maintaining a diverse membership, including special programs to promote interest and develop expertise in the next generation of foreign policy leaders;

- convening meetings at its headquarters in New York and in Washington, DC, and other cities where senior government officials, members of Congress, global leaders, and prominent thinkers come together with CFR members to discuss and debate major international issues;

- supporting a Studies Program that fosters independent research, enabling CFR scholars to produce articles, reports, and books and hold roundtables that analyze foreign policy issues and make concrete policy recommendations;

- publishing *Foreign Affairs*, the preeminent journal of international affairs and U.S. foreign policy;

- sponsoring Independent Task Forces that produce reports with both findings and policy prescriptions on the most important foreign policy topics; and

- providing up-to-date information and analysis about world events and American foreign policy on its website, CFR.org.

Letter From the Chair

Chairman
David M. Rubenstein

The Council on Foreign Relations is a unique and vital institution. Founded in 1921 in the aftermath of World War I, the Council has provided an unrivaled forum for thoughtful debate on America's role in the world for almost one hundred years. A hybrid institution—a think tank, membership organization, venue for meetings, educator, and publisher—the Council is dedicated to being an independent, nonpartisan resource to help people better understand the world and the foreign policy choices facing the United States.

To continue to serve this mission effectively over the next century, the Council's financial future must be secure. Membership dues cover less than 10 percent of CFR's annual budget. Annual giving, though generous, provides roughly 15 percent of the budget. The Council takes no money from governments, and funding from foundations can be unpredictable. For the Council to remain independent and nonpartisan, it must be able to set its own agenda and be a forum for free and independent expression. Furthermore, expanding the Council's outreach beyond its traditional elite constituency—essential in order to involve more voices in the foreign policy discussion—requires substantial new investments.

Recognizing this, CFR embarked on an ambitious capital campaign beginning in 2014 to help secure the Council's second century. The Council at 100 Campaign set a goal of raising $150 million in new gifts and I am pleased to report that the campaign well exceeded this goal. The campaign concluded in July, surpassing $180 million in gifts and pledges. This is a significant achievement, especially considering that the campaign counted only those gifts made over and above the Council's regular fundraising. Gifts from current and former members of the Council's Board of Directors were particularly generous, constituting more than half of the campaign's total contributions.

Campaign gifts will help support and expand nearly every aspect of the Council. Approximately 60 percent was committed toward the Council's endowment, where it will grow and provide the Council with a sound foundation of long-term financial support. The remainder will provide operating funds

Vice Chairman
Blair Effron

Vice Chairman
Jami Miscik

to grow CFR's education initiative, broaden its outreach to new constituencies, and support technology upgrades.

Other gifts established three new endowed chairs in U.S. foreign policy, emerging technologies and national security, and global governance, as well as senior fellowships in international economics, Asia studies, and business and foreign policy. The Stephen M. Kellen Term Member Program was also strengthened, and we received a gift to endow a fully paid internship program. Annual lectures on refugee and migration policy and economic growth and foreign policy were funded, and new International Affairs Fellowships in Canada, India, and international economics launched. Finally, more than $25 million was given in support of CFR's Education Program.

The campaign was remarkably successful, but continued support from CFR's members is as crucial as ever. The challenges facing this nation and the world—from trade disputes and migration to the rise of populism and nationalism—highlight more than ever the need for an independent and nonpartisan voice in the debate. Working together, we can ensure the Council remains that voice in the century to come. We are indebted to the Campaign Working Group, which helped ensure the success of this initiative, and extend a particular thanks to Richard Haass for his tireless efforts. Thank you to all who have contributed to the campaign. And thank you for your continued support of the Council.

President's Message

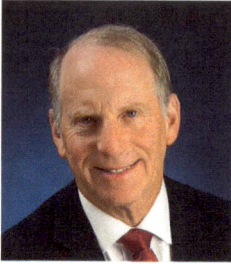

President
Richard N. Haass

There was no shortage of foreign policy issues to cover this year. Whether it was the deteriorating situations in Venezuela or Sudan, the assassination of Jamal Khashoggi, rising tensions between the United States and both Iran and Russia, the stops and starts of negotiations with China and North Korea, or the never-ending saga of Brexit, events shifted seemingly by the minute. The world at the beginning of each day was rarely the same by day's end.

The speed with which history now unfolds requires the Council to be more agile than ever. The quantity and complexity of the global problems facing us have produced a nearly insatiable appetite among experts and citizens alike for timely, rigorous analysis that helps to make sense of all that is going on. One way the Council meets this challenge is through its online presence on two websites: CFR.org and ForeignAffairs.com.

Explanatory content is the foundation of CFR.org. The website now features nearly six hundred Backgrounders—succinct yet authoritative explainers of fewer than two thousand words produced by CFR.org's editorial team that introduce readers to important issues, ranging from tariffs and immigration to NATO and the role of the International Criminal Court, and often include charts, maps, timelines, and other graphics. Backgrounders are intended to be "evergreen" resources, maintaining their relevancy well past their original publication date. Backgrounders help serve the Council's educational mission and have been incorporated into numerous college and graduate school syllabi.

To complement Backgrounders, CFR.org recently launched a new, shorter-format feature, In Brief. These products, approximately five hundred words and authored by senior fellows and editorial staff, offer an initial take on the most pressing issues and events. Because they cover developing stories, In Briefs also often include predictions about how issues will evolve and, in some cases, recommendations for policy. In Briefs have covered recent elections in India, Israel, and South Africa, and explored emerging issues such as Indonesia's growing religious divide and possible U.S. sanctions on the Muslim Brotherhood.

Another notable franchise from CFR.org is its award-winning series of InfoGuides. To date, the Council has produced ten in-depth narrative pieces that explain complex international challenges through a combination of videos, photos, interactive timelines, and other data visualizations. This series is the successor to CFR's groundbreaking Crisis Guide interactives. The Council has now won four Emmy Awards for guides on Iran, the global economy, Darfur, and deforestation in the Amazon. Our two most recent InfoGuides have addressed modern slavery and the global refugee crisis.

CFR.org also produces two podcasts. *The World Next Week*, created in 2007 and hosted by Director of Studies James M. Lindsay and Managing Editor Robert McMahon, previews the coming week's major foreign policy–related events in a conversational style. In addition, *The President's Inbox* features interviews between Lindsay and an expert guest on a wide range of global issues. Podcasts are a critical way of reaching younger audiences, and the Council will expand on these offerings in the coming year. A new podcast, *Why It Matters*, will offer shorter, twenty-five-minute explorations of a significant country or issue in the news. Episodes will feature expert interviews but will be narrative based, with the host walking the listener through a larger story and helping to clarify difficult concepts for those new to the foreign policy discussion.

The Council also has fourteen blogs authored by senior fellows covering the waterfront of foreign policy issues. Other noteworthy digital content from senior fellows this year includes a Women's Workplace Equality Index, a Belt and Road Tracker, a microsite dedicated to understanding proposed changes to Japan's constitution, and two interactives on the relationships between health and democracy and health and urbanization.

In addition to posting original content, CFR.org curates the best foreign policy analysis from any source or institution and helps disseminate it to the CFR audience. The site's homepage features rotating packages of articles and other resources centered on trending issues; the *Daily News Brief*, a newsletter published each weekday featuring a roundup

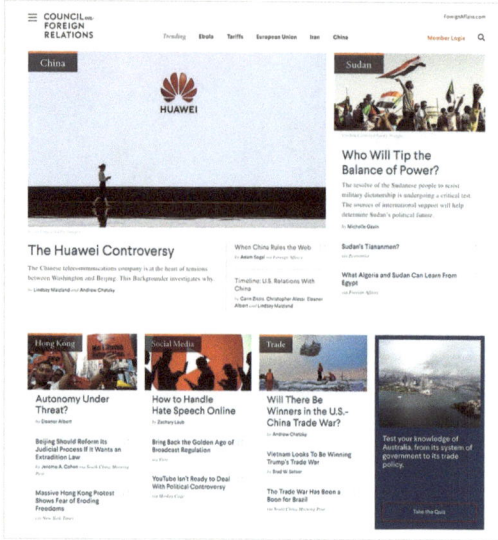

Left: CFR.org homepage on June 12, 2019.
Right: ForeignAffairs.com homepage on June 12, 2019.

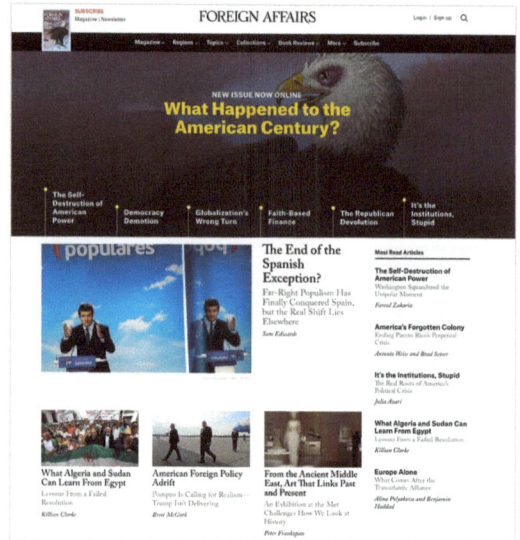

of news from across the globe, helps some forty thousand foreign policy professionals and others stay abreast of the latest international developments and the best resources for understanding them. Finally, the Council holds approximately 125 on-the-record meetings each year, all available on CFR.org and the Council's YouTube channel.

Both *Foreign Affairs* and its website, ForeignAffairs.com, also play an important role. Although the magazine's bimonthly print issues focus mostly on the underlying forces driving the headlines, ForeignAffairs.com offers timely but in-depth commentary on the latest foreign policy challenges.

Since its launch in 2009, ForeignAffairs.com has greatly expanded its offerings. The site publishes approximately three hundred online-only articles annually. These articles are slightly shorter than those that appear in the magazine's print issue, but they are no less rigorous.

The website also features digital anthologies focused on major foreign policy questions and comprising relevant *Foreign Affairs* articles, as well as reading lists curated by *Foreign Affairs* editors. In addition, the This Day in History series helps contextualize current events by highlighting historical anniversaries and *Foreign Affairs* articles about those critical moments

in history. The website also offers nearly eight hundred audio articles, and the magazine will be launching its own podcast in the coming year.

The world can be hard to understand. Global issues are complex and the sheer number of countries and entities interacting at once makes it difficult to follow events, much less predict how things will play out. We cannot make foreign policy any less challenging, but on CFR.org and ForeignAffairs.com we can present the issues in a way that is timely, relevant, and accessible, setting forth the stakes and policy considerations. Doing so is vital to ensure an informed citizenry.

Richard N. Haass
President

Top: *Montana Governor Steve Bullock, former Secretary of Commerce Penny Pritzker, and CFR President Richard N. Haass discuss the future of work at the National Governors Association 2019 Winter Meeting in Washington, DC.*

Bottom: *Canadian Minister of International Trade Diversification Jim Carr, Minister of Foreign Affairs Chrystia Freeland, Prime Minister Justin Trudeau, and CFR President Richard N. Haass discuss Canada's global outlook at the Russell C. Leffingwell Lecture.*

2019
Highlights

Website Stats

Audience grew to

16.8M

users (up 96.6%)

Online sessions went up

52.6%

Page views increased

23%

New Fellows

Jonathan J. Finer
adjunct senior fellow for U.S. foreign policy

Thomas E. Graham
distinguished fellow

Martin S. Indyk
distinguished fellow

Mira Rapp-Hooper
senior fellow for Asia studies

4
new books published in FY 2019

Model Diplomacy Stats

Nearly

35,000 students

in all 50 states and in more than 100 countries have used MD since 2016

More than

2.2M

YouTube views in FY 2019

Meetings held in

18

cities across the United States and around the world

an average of

271

educators and students per call

Academic Conference Calls

an average of

42

schools represented on each call

Meetings

The Council on Foreign Relations provides a nonpartisan forum for thoughtful and informed foreign policy debate, drawing leaders and experts in government, business, the media, and academia for discussions with members on critical issues in foreign policy and international relations.

This year, CFR welcomed dozens of current and former heads of state, foreign officials, and leaders of international organizations. Beginning with the opening of the seventy-third session of the UN General Assembly in September, CFR hosted the presidents of Botswana, Chile, the Democratic Republic of Congo, Kosovo, South Africa, and South Korea; prime ministers of Canada, Malaysia, and Spain; chief executive of Afghanistan; vice president of Nigeria; deputy prime minister of Qatar; foreign ministers of Canada, China, Greece, Iran, Jordan, Oman, Saudi Arabia, and the United Arab Emirates; and central bank governors of France and Italy. CFR also hosted the managing director of the International Monetary Fund; chief executive of the World Bank; director general of the World Trade Organization; UN high commissioner for human rights; UN high commissioner for refugees; UN Development Program administrator; deputy secretary-general of the North Atlantic Treaty Organization; a former UN secretary-general; former presidents of Colombia, Ireland, and Liberia; and former prime ministers of Italy and the United Kingdom.

Current and former U.S. officials also spoke at CFR, among them Federal Reserve Chair Jerome Powell; FBI Director Christopher Wray; Secretary of Homeland Security Kirstjen Nielsen; Council of Economic Advisers Chairman Kevin Hassett; Senators Chris Coons, Joni Ernst, Ed Markey, Chris Murphy, Chris Van Hollen, and Mark Warner; Representatives Eliot Engel, Jim Jordan, Michael McCaul, Adam Schiff, and Mac Thornberry; Washington Governor Jay Inslee; USAID Administrator Mark Green; President and CEO of the Federal Reserve Bank of New York John Williams; former Federal Reserve Chairs Ben Bernanke and Alan Greenspan; former Treasury Secretaries Timothy Geithner, Jacob Lew, and Henry Paulson; and former Secretary of State John Kerry.

CFR held several multi-session symposia this year that offered members deep dives into topics such as the lessons and legacy of the global financial crisis ten years later, leveling the economic playing field for women, artificial intelligence and disinformation, health and globalization, the status of democracy around the world, and how behavioral economics can address global poverty. In addition, the Lessons From History series looked at the twenty-fifth anniversaries of the Oslo Accords and the end of apartheid in South Africa, the fortieth anniversary of the Iranian Revolution, the legacy of the Jimmy Carter administration, and presidential leadership.

As part of its Daughters and Sons series, which invites members to bring their high school– and college-age children to experience a CFR meeting, the Council hosted CFR Distinguished Fellow and former U.S. Ambassador to Israel Martin S. Indyk, former Secretary of Health and Human Services and American University President Sylvia Mathews Burwell, VisionSpring founder Jordan Kassalow and Rabbi Jennifer Krause, and historian Jill Lepore. The CEO Speaker series brought Morgan Stanley Chairman and CEO James Gorman, NYU Langone Health CEO Robert Grossman, and Visa CEO Al Kelly to CFR.

CFR also launched two new meeting series: Young Professionals Briefings, for individuals who have completed their undergraduate studies but have not yet reached the age of thirty to be eligible for term membership, and Distinguished Voices, which features prominent individuals reflecting on their careers and involvement in a critical juncture in the history of the country or the world. Additionally, CFR continued the popular salon dinner series, in which members meet with one another to discuss pressing foreign policy issues.

More than three hundred term members gathered in Washington in November for the twenty-third annual Term Member Conference, which featured a keynote discussion with General Lori J. Robinson, the first female combat commander in the U.S. Air Force. CFR also organized several term member trips, including one in May to El Paso, Texas, where participants got a firsthand look at the situation on the U.S.-Mexico border.

Finally, in April, CFR hosted the seventh annual Conference on Diversity in International Affairs. The conference, a collaborative effort by CFR, the Global Access Pipeline, and the International Career Advancement Program, brought together more than three hundred students and mid-career professionals from diverse backgrounds historically underrepresented in the foreign policy field for sessions on foreign policy, professional development, global skills–building, and career opportunities in international affairs. Council member Stacey Abrams, former minority leader of the Georgia House of Representatives, gave the keynote address.

Top left: President of South Africa Cyril Ramaphosa discusses his administration's domestic and international agendas.

Top right: Managing Director of the International Monetary Fund Christine Lagarde gives keynote remarks at the Women and the Law: Leveling the Economic Playing Field symposium.

Bottom: FBI Director Christopher Wray and CFR President Richard N. Haass discuss the FBI's role in protecting the United States from today's threats.

National Program

The National Program connects the plurality of CFR members who live outside New York and Washington, DC, with CFR and its resources. This year, the National Program hosted discussions in eighteen cities across the United States and around the world on topics including the U.S.-China trade war, the future of the transatlantic alliance, U.S. policy toward Saudi Arabia, and the crisis in Venezuela. CFR also held interactive conference calls and offered livestreams and teleconferences of meetings in New York and Washington, DC.

In December, more than two hundred participants from across the country and around the world convened at the fourth annual National Symposium in Menlo Park, California, to discuss issues at the intersection of foreign policy and technology. Former National Security Advisor H. R. McMaster was the keynote speaker; other sessions covered the U.S.-China innovation race and biotechnology and the health-care revolution.

As always, the year ended with the National Conference in New York, which convened over four hundred participants for three days of panels and discussions. Speakers included Speaker of the House Nancy Pelosi and former Mayor of New York City Michael Bloomberg.

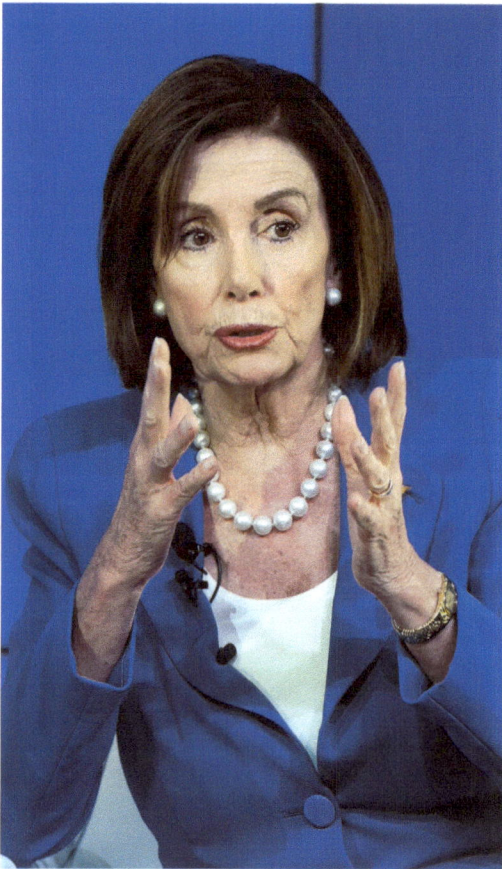

Left: *Speaker of the U.S. House of Representatives Nancy Pelosi discusses foreign affairs and the current state of politics at the National Conference in New York.*

Right: *Former National Security Advisor to the White House H. R. McMaster speaks at the National Symposium in Menlo Park, California.*

Corporate Program

CFR's Corporate Program provides member companies from across the globe access to CFR's experts, research, and meetings to help them better understand the international issues that affect their businesses. This year, the program held meetings and roundtables on issues including China's Belt and Road Initiative, sanctions, student debt, and arms control. CFR also held conference calls to provide executives timely analysis on Brexit, President Donald J. Trump's threat to impose tariffs on Mexico, European Parliament elections, and the U.S.-Mexico-Canada Agreement.

The annual Corporate Conference in April featured a keynote conversation with JPMorgan Chase Chairman and CEO Jamie Dimon as well as sessions on trade and economic nationalism, geopolitical risk, and the effects of artificial intelligence on productivity and wage growth. CFR also hosted the inaugural CEO Summit, which brought a select group of CEOs of corporate member companies to the Council for a half day of discussions on the global economy, geopolitics, and the role of business in society.

JPMorgan Chase Chairman and CEO Jamie Dimon reflects on his career, the role of business in public policy, and global markets with CFR Chairman David M. Rubenstein at CFR's Corporate Conference.

The David Rockefeller Studies Program

The Studies Program, CFR's think tank, analyzes pressing global challenges and offers recommendations for policymakers in the United States and elsewhere. CFR's research aims to be more policy relevant than that of most universities and more rigorous than what many advocacy groups produce.

CFR experts published four books this year. Books reflect the emphasis CFR places on in-depth research and analysis. In *Plagues and the Paradox of Progress: Why the World Is Getting Healthier in Worrisome Ways*, Thomas J. Bollyky, senior fellow for global health, economics, and development and director of the Global Health program, argues that though the global population is getting healthier and living longer, the recent hard-won gains in health are bringing a host of new and destabilizing problems, including a rise in noncommunicable diseases. In *The Empty Throne: America's Abdication of Global Leadership*, Senior Vice President, Director of Studies, and Maurice R. Greenberg Chair James Lindsay and Ivo Daalder, president of the Chicago Council on Global Affairs, argue that President Trump's America First policies have focused on beating rather than leading America's friends and allies, in the process weakening long-term U.S. security and prosperity. In *Japan Rearmed: The Politics of Military Power*, Senior Fellow for Japan Studies Sheila A. Smith argues that Japan, by rethinking its commitment to pacifism, is not only responding to increasing threats from North Korean missiles and Chinese maritime activities but also reevaluating its security dependence on the United States. Finally, in *How We Win: How Cutting-Edge Entrepreneurs, Political Visionaries, Enlightened Business Leaders, and Social Media Mavens Can Defeat the Extremist Threat*, Adjunct Senior Fellow Farah Pandith argues that governments acting alone are losing the war against violent extremism and that

collaboration with other actors in society is essential to counter this threat.

Several previously published books by senior fellows received recognition this year. *The Road Not Taken: Edward Lansdale and the American Tragedy in Vietnam* by Max Boot, Jeane J. Kirkpatrick senior fellow for national security studies, was named a finalist for the 2019 Pulitzer Prize in biography; *The Marshall Plan: Dawn of the Cold War* by Benn Steil, senior fellow and director of international economics, won the New-York Historical Society's Barbara and David Zalaznick Book Prize; and *The Third Revolution: Xi Jinping and the New Chinese State* by Elizabeth C. Economy, C. V. Starr senior fellow and director for Asia studies, was short-listed for the Lionel Gelber Prize.

In Council Special Reports, CFR experts provide timely responses to developing crises and contributions to current policy dilemmas. In *Trump's Foreign Policies Are Better Than They Seem*, Robert D. Blackwill, Henry A. Kissinger senior fellow for U.S. foreign policy, argues that the president's realist approach to dealing with China and the greater Middle East warrants higher marks for his foreign policy overall than many of his critics are willing to concede. In *Neither Friend Nor Foe: The Future of U.S.-Turkey Relations*, Steven A. Cook, Eni Enrico Mattei senior fellow for Middle East and Africa studies, argues that the strategic relationship between the United States and Turkey is over and that the United States should develop military alternatives to using Incirlik Air Base, continue to cooperate with the Kurdish People's Protection Units in Syria, and publicly oppose Turkish policies that undermine U.S. interests. In *Zero Botnets: Building a Global Effort to Clean Up the Internet*, Whitney Shepardson Senior Fellow Robert K. Knake and Jason Healey, senior research scholar at Columbia University, warn that the threat of botnets to the internet

Senior Fellow for Global Health, Economics, and Development and Director of the Global Health Program Thomas J. Bollyky addresses the audience at an event to discuss his book Plagues and the Paradox of Progress: Why the World Is Getting Healthier in Worrisome Ways.

is too great to ignore; nations and international institutions, they argue, should work to establish the principle that states are responsible for the harm that botnets based within their borders cause to others. Further, they assert, when governments are unable or unwilling to be responsible, other states may be justified in taking action to thwart cross-border effects.

In December, the Center for Preventive Action, which aims to help policymakers devise timely and practical strategies to prevent and mitigate armed conflict around the world, published the eleventh annual *Preventive Priorities Survey*. Five hundred foreign policy experts evaluated which conflicts around the world might escalate and harm U.S. interests in 2019. Top concerns include a highly disruptive cyberattack on U.S. critical infrastructure, renewed tensions on the Korean Peninsula following a collapse of negotiations, and an armed confrontation between the United States and Iran.

Policy Innovation Memoranda address critical problems where new, creative thinking is needed. In "Defending America From Foreign Election Interference," Max Boot and Max Bergmann, senior fellow at the Center for American Progress, argue that to protect U.S. elections from foreign interference, the United States should create an entirely new agency to safeguard elections and promptly sanction and possibly retaliate in kind against countries that interfere with elections. In "Rethinking U.S. Policy Toward the Palestinians," Philip H. Gordon, Mary and David Boies senior fellow in U.S. foreign policy, argues that the Trump administration's current policy is counterproductive to the prospects of reaching peace with Israel and the administration should forgo introducing a comprehensive peace plan and instead take steps toward improving conditions on the ground and preserving prospects for more ambitious agreements. In "Increasing Female Participation in Peacekeeping Operations," Jamille Bigio, senior fellow for Women and Foreign Policy, and Rachel Vogelstein, Douglas Dillon senior fellow and director of the Women and Foreign Policy program, argue that because female participation has been shown to improve intelligence about potential

security risks and dispute resolution as well as reduce the risk of sexual exploitation, the U.S. government should encourage the United Nations to adopt policies that would spur countries to increase the training and deployment of female peacekeepers.

Cyber Briefs address emerging cybersecurity challenges. In "A New Old Threat: Countering the Return of Chinese Industrial Cyber Espionage," Adam Segal, Ira A. Lipman chair in emerging technologies and national security and director of the Digital and Cyberspace Policy program, and Lorand Laskai, CFR research associate, recommend that to counter intellectual property theft by China, the United States should build a multinational coalition to coordinate attribution of Chinese hackers, sanction Chinese companies, and strengthen cyber defenses and counterintelligence.

The think tank welcomed several new fellows this year, including Jonathan J. Finer, former chief of staff and director of policy planning at the U.S. Department of State (2015–2017), who joined as an adjunct senior fellow for U.S. foreign policy; Thomas E. Graham, former special assistant to the president and senior director for Russia on the National Security Council staff (2004–2007), as a distinguished fellow focusing on Russian and Eurasian affairs; Martin Indyk, former special envoy for the Israeli-Palestinian negotiations and former ambassador to Israel (1995–1997 and 2000–2001), as a distinguished fellow specializing in the Middle East; and Mira Rapp-Hooper, previously a lecturer and a senior research scholar at Yale Law School, as a senior fellow for Asia studies.

Top: *Vice President and Deputy Director of Studies Shannon K. O'Neil; Senior Fellows Edward Alden and Brad W. Setser; and CFR President Richard N. Haass speak on a panel at CFR's Annual Dinner in New York.*

Bottom: *Senior Vice President, Director of Studies, and Maurice R. Greenberg Chair James M. Lindsay addresses the audience at a panel to discuss his book* The Empty Throne: America's Abdication of Global Leadership.

Senior Fellow for Japan Studies Sheila A. Smith speaks on a panel about her book Japan Rearmed: The Politics of Military Power.

Council of Councils

Task Forces

This year, the Council of Councils (CoC), a consortium of twenty-eight leading think tanks from around the world that convenes biannually to discuss the state of global governance and how to improve it, held meetings in Seoul and Washington, DC. U.S. Special Representative for Venezuela Elliott Abrams (on leave from his senior fellow post at CFR) addressed the group at the eighth annual conference in Washington. The CoC also released its annual Report Card on International Cooperation, which evaluates global efforts on ten issues. The group gave international cooperation a C grade overall, a slight upgrade from last year's C-, and rated mitigating and adapting to climate change as the top global priority in 2019.

CFR's Independent Task Force Program convenes diverse and distinguished groups of experts who offer analysis of and policy prescriptions for major foreign policy issues facing the United States. The Independent Task Force report *The Work Ahead: Machines, Skills, and U.S. Leadership in the Twenty-First Century*, released in April 2018, served as the inspiration for the "Vice Special Report: The Future of Work," which premiered on HBO a year later, in April 2019.

A new Task Force examining the state of U.S. technological innovation given growing domestic and international challenges, including increased competition from China, launched this year. The report will be released in the fall of 2019.

East Asia Institute President Yul Sohn delivers opening remarks at the Council of Councils Eleventh Regional Conference in Seoul.

Education

CFR's educational initiative aims to provide every student with the skills and knowledge about the world to prepare them for a wide range of careers and ensure an informed citizenry. Model Diplomacy, the National Security Council simulation program launched in 2016, continues to add new features. CFR broadened its offerings this year by developing a stand-alone UN Security Council simulation, an infectious disease case for use at schools of public health, and new "basic" versions of existing cases tailored for younger students. Nearly thirty-five thousand students in all fifty states and in more than one hundred countries have used Model Diplomacy.

The first unit of World101—the online modular course that focuses on the fundamental concepts of international relations and foreign policy—has formally launched. Global Era Issues includes primers featuring videos, interactive timelines, and data visualizations on issues such as globalization, terrorism, climate change, and migration. Each module is designed to help learners inside and out of traditional classrooms grasp critical concepts and understand their relevance. Subsequent units of World101 will be released over the coming year.

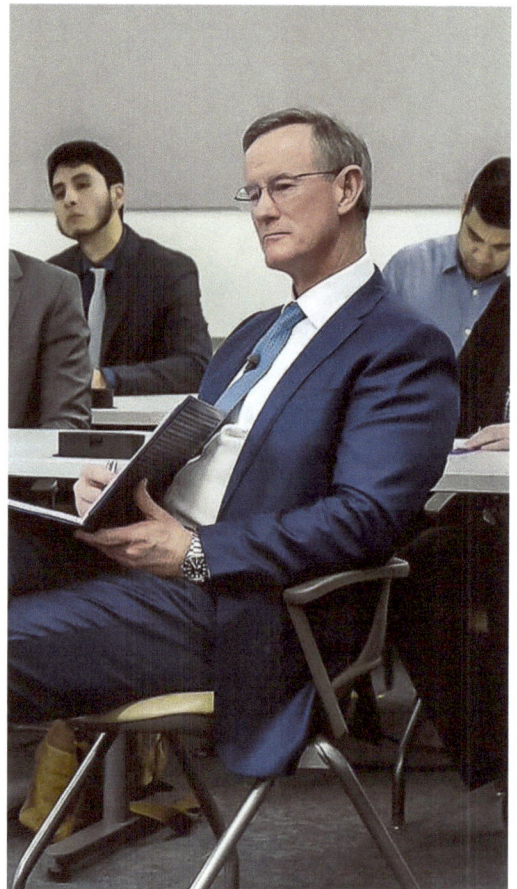

Left: *More than three hundred students joined the ninth annual Back-to-School event, "Responses to the Global Refugee Crisis."*
Right: *Admiral William H. McRaven conducts a Model Diplomacy simulation in his classroom at University of Texas, Austin.*

Outreach

Academic Outreach

CFR connects educators and students with CFR publications, digital educational products, and programming for teaching and learning about international affairs.

The Academic Conference Call series provides a forum for educators and students to interact with CFR experts and scholars and participate in the debate on foreign policy issues. This year, calls covered U.S. economic security and the future of work, Congress's role in foreign policy, mental health on campus, U.S. relations in the Gulf, the future of the European Union, and international security under changing climate conditions. Former Secretary of State Madeleine Albright also led a call on the rise of authoritarian nationalism. Calls averaged nearly three hundred participants from more than forty schools.

The annual College and University Educators Workshop, which convenes professors for discussions on pressing global issues and to share best practices for teaching international affairs, brought more than one hundred professors from thirty-six states and Canada to the Council. Sessions covered the global outlook, counterterrorism efforts, teaching with CFR resources, and the economic gains of gender parity.

Religion and Foreign Policy Program

CFR's Religion and Foreign Policy (RFP) program advances understanding of the forces shaping international relations through exchange between faith leaders and policymakers. Constituents include clergy, community leaders, seminary heads, scholars of religion, and representatives of faith-based organizations. Through its nonpartisan, authoritative resources and analysis, CFR informs their work and fosters dialogue within their communities.

This year, the program held roundtables and conference calls on U.S. immigration policy, religious persecution in China, the geopolitical implications of the Ukrainian Orthodox Church's split from the Russian patriarchate, democracy and authoritarianism in Brazil, the pope's historic visit to the United Arab Emirates, peace and politics in South Asia, the twentieth anniversary of the U.S. International Religious Freedom Act, and the release of the U.S. government's Fourth National Climate Assessment.

In June, the thirteenth annual Religion and Foreign Policy Workshop brought together nearly 130 congregational and lay leaders, religion scholars, and representatives of faith-based organizations from thirty-five religious traditions for a conversation with U.S. Ambassador-at-Large Samuel D. Brownback and discussions on social change in sub-Saharan Africa, U.S. involvement in the Middle East, and combating climate change.

Washington Outreach

CFR's Congress and U.S. Foreign Policy program aims to connect the work of the Council with members of Congress, their staffs, and executive branch officials. The program is an essential source of independent, nonpartisan analysis that informs the direction of U.S. foreign policy. It also offers a unique forum in which policymakers from both sides of the aisle can come together for all-too-rare reasoned discussions on foreign policy issues.

This year, CFR fellows were called to testify before Congress five times, and the program held 265 roundtables and briefings for members of Congress and their staffs. CFR fellows and staff have also been a resource for the executive branch, briefing officials from the Departments of State, Treasury, and Defense; National Security Council; Office of the Vice President; U.S. Agency for International Development; and various elements of the intelligence community.

CFR also continued its House and Senate principals breakfast series, cohosted with former Senate Majority Leader Thomas A. Daschle and former Representative Vin Weber. The series brings together representatives and senators for an in-depth examination of a critical foreign policy issue. The first breakfast of the 116th Congress featured a conversation with former National Security Advisors Stephen Hadley and Susan Rice; subsequent discussions this year covered North Korea and Venezuela.

In March, more than two hundred Council members and congressional staff attended CFR's Capitol Hill reception. This gathering allows CFR members and staff to interact with members of Congress and their staffs in an informal setting and provides an opportunity for members of Congress to socialize with one another. In addition, members of the Congressional Foreign Policy Study Group, a selective program for senior-level congressional staff, traveled to New York in September to meet with CFR and *Foreign Affairs* experts.

State and Local Outreach

CFR's State and Local Officials initiative provides programming and resources for elected representatives and their staffs at the city and state levels. The initiative features a conference call series on pressing global issues that affect local agendas, showcases Council experts at major gatherings of state and local leaders, and connects officials with CFR publications, including *Foreign Affairs*.

This year, Bernard L. Schwartz Senior Fellow Edward Alden led briefings for the National Governors Association (NGA) and U.S. Conference of Mayors on the CFR Independent Task Force report on the future of work. CFR President Richard Haass and former Secretary of Commerce Penny Pritzker (co-chair of the Task Force) also spoke about the future of work on a panel alongside Montana Governor Steve Bullock at the NGA Winter Meeting. In May, Senior Fellow Elizabeth Economy briefed governors and senior staffers on the dynamics of the U.S.-China relationship prior to the fifth annual U.S.-China Governors' Collaboration Summit.

Local Journalists Initiative

This year, CFR launched a new initiative to reach locally based journalists and equip them with the resources and best practices needed to introduce a global dimension to their reporting on local issues. As part of this initiative, and with the help of a grant from the John S. and James L. Knight Foundation, CFR held a pilot workshop in New York in January, which brought together nearly one hundred locally based print, digital, and broadcast journalists from across the United States and Canada for discussions with CFR fellows and other experts. The workshop included a conversation on the state of U.S. foreign policy and the media with CNN's Fareed Zakaria.

Facing top: CFR President Richard N. Haass (right) in conversation with Harvard University President Lawrence S. Bacow at the American Council on Education's Annual Meeting in Philadelphia.

Facing bottom: Senior Fellow for Energy and the Environment and Director of the Program on Energy Security and Climate Change Amy M. Jaffe speaks at the House Appropriations Committee's Subcommittee on Energy and Water Development.

CFR Digital

CFR.org continues to be a leading source of timely analysis on critical foreign policy issues. The website's most popular pieces of content are Backgrounders, which introduce readers to important topics ranging from the crisis in Venezuela to the opioid epidemic. New Backgrounders produced this year covered tariffs, China's crackdown on the Uighurs, global comparisons of inequality and tax rates, Made in China 2025, the role of the International Criminal Court, and the Huawei controversy. The website also offers fourteen blogs authored by senior fellows, interviews, expert briefs, digital interactives, and numerous other resources. CFR.org saw extraordinary growth in traffic. Its audience grew to 16.8 million users, a 96.6 percent increase from last fiscal year. Online sessions increased 52.6 percent and page views increased 23 percent from 2018. Growth was particularly strong among users who came through search engines, indicating that Google and other search engines increasingly regard CFR.org as a trusted resource.

In February, CFR.org released the latest in its award-winning series of InfoGuides. "No Refuge: Why Refugees Have Shrinking Options" explores the underpinnings of the world's refugee crisis. The guide provides an overview of the postwar international refugee system and covers conflicts such as violence and state failure in Latin America, expulsions of the Rohingya in Myanmar, and the civil war in Syria. The guide also chronicles the role of rising anti-immigrant policies that have led to reductions in the number of refugees accepted by developed countries.

CFR also launched a weekly feature, CFR Quizzes, designed to promote a greater understanding of foreign policy and international relations. These ten-question quizzes offered short but deep dives into countries, issues, and historical events. The answers were much more than just right or wrong—they gave context and explanations that helped make the quizzes an educational asset in or out of the classroom.

Other notable online interactive reports produced this year include the Women's Workplace Equality Index from the Women and Foreign Policy program, which features the first global index ranking countries on gender equality in the workplace; a micro-site led by Senior Fellow Sheila Smith on the historic referendum Prime Minister Shinzo Abe is calling for to amend the Japanese constitution; a Belt and Road Tracker by Senior Fellow Benn Steil and Analyst Benjamin Della Rocca that traces sixty-seven countries' bilateral economic relationships with China over time; and a series of interactives from Senior Fellow Thomas Bollyky on the relationships between health and democracy and health and urbanization.

The Council also launched a redesigned online member services portal in December. The portal provides an improved user experience for CFR members by better highlighting member events, making registration for events easier, and facilitating more fluid communication among members. It also incorporates two-factor authentication to better protect members' data and privacy.

In addition, CFR maintains a significant presence on social media. The Council's institutional accounts have more than 415,000 followers on Facebook, over 402,000 followers on Twitter, more than 100,000 followers on LinkedIn, and over 11,000 followers on Instagram. When including the pages of individual scholars and programs, the Council reaches 1.5 million people on Twitter and 516,000 on Facebook. The Council's YouTube channel has more than 84,000 subscribers, and videos of CFR meetings and other content have received more than 15.3 million views.

No Refuge
A CFR Infoguide

COUNCIL *on*
FOREIGN
RELATIONS

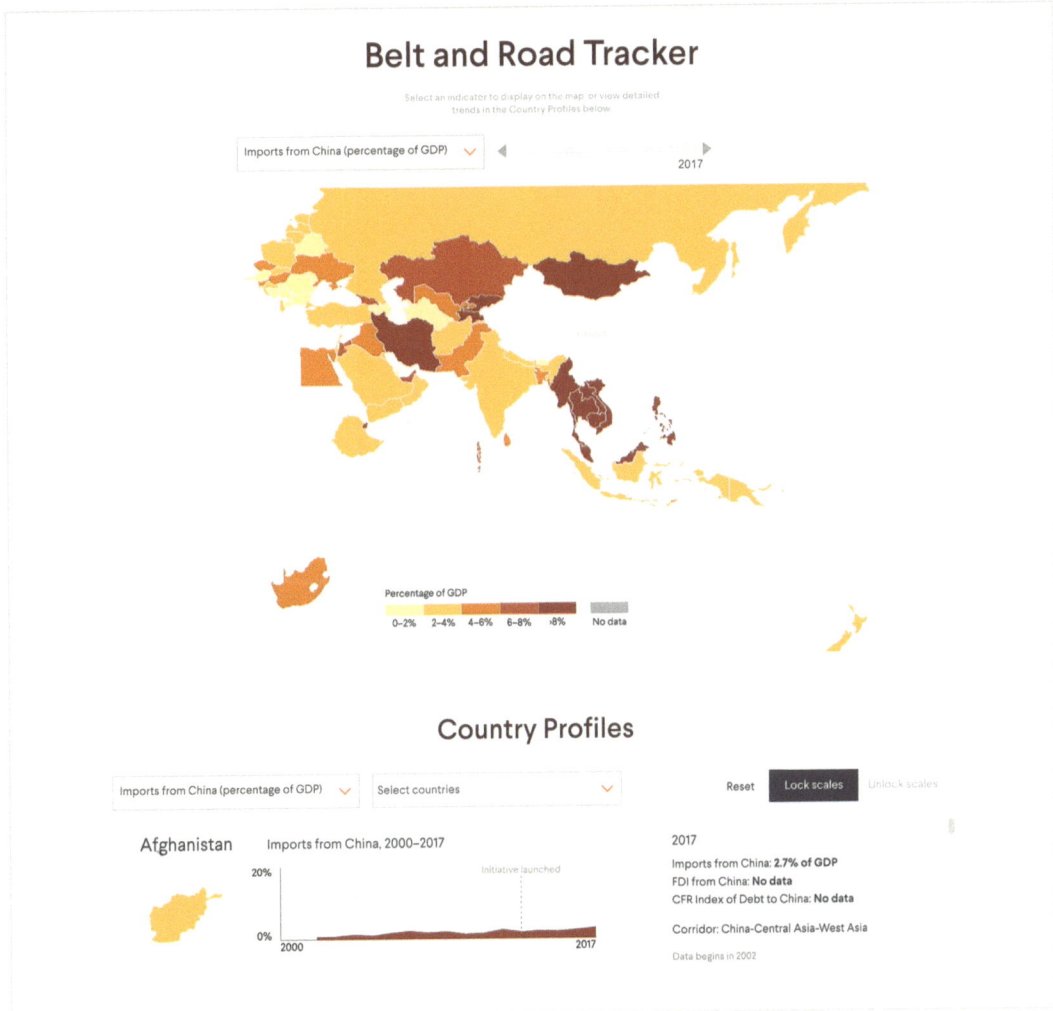

Belt and Road Tracker

Select an indicator to display on the map or view detailed
trends in the Country Profiles below

Imports from China (percentage of GDP) ∨   ◀   ▶
                                                                    2017

Percentage of GDP

0–2%   2–4%   4–6%   6–8%   >8%   No data

Country Profiles

Imports from China (percentage of GDP) ∨   Select countries ∨   Reset   Lock scales   Unlock scales

Afghanistan   Imports from China, 2000–2017

20%   Initiative launched

0%
   2000   2017

2017
Imports from China: **2.7% of GDP**
FDI from China: **No data**
CFR Index of Debt to China: **No data**

Corridor: China-Central Asia-West Asia

Data begins in 2002

Top: *A CFR InfoGuide explores the challenges facing global refugees.*
Bottom: *A CFR interactive on China's Belt and Road Initiative.*

Foreign Affairs

Foreign Affairs magazine is one of the most thoughtful, read, and influential in the field. The magazine complements all else the Council does by providing a space for long-form analysis from a broad pool of expert voices. Each print issue includes a lead package on a consequential issue, complemented by in-depth analysis of other challenges. In addition, ForeignAffairs.com offers daily commentary on the latest foreign policy developments.

Lead packages in the magazine this year explored competing characterizations of the world we are living in, the battle to shape the future of cyberspace, nuclear weapons, different notions of world order, nationalism, the future of American foreign policy, and the end of American primacy. The magazine also published notable pieces by Secretary of State Mike Pompeo on Iran, Senator Elizabeth Warren on a progressive U.S. foreign policy, and former Treasury Secretary Larry Summers and former Council of Economic Advisers Chairman Jason Furman on the need to rethink budget deficits.

ForeignAffairs.com recently hit an all-time high in traffic. Highlights on the website included pieces by Georgetown Professor Daniel Nexon on the foreign policy debate on the American left, historian Margaret MacMillan on the lessons of 1919 for the present, Florida International University Professor Frank O. Mora on what a U.S. military intervention in Venezuela would look like, and University of Kentucky Professor George C. Herring on the lessons the United States can learn from Vietnam as it considers leaving Afghanistan.

Finally, the magazine transitioned to a new fulfillment house in December and released its first iOS and Android mobile apps. *Foreign Affairs* also held issue launches in New York and Washington and partnered with the *Wall Street Journal*, *Scientific American*, and Intelligence Squared for other events.

Former Undersecretary of Defense for Policy at the Department of Defense Michèle Flournoy, Chair in Emerging Technologies and National Security and Director of the Digital and Cyberspace Policy program Adam Segal, and Foreign Affairs *Editor Gideon Rose address the audience at the September/October 2018* Foreign Affairs *issue launch in Washington, DC.*

Membership

Membership

Since its founding in 1921, the Council on Foreign Relations has grown a membership of more than five thousand prominent leaders in the foreign policy arena, including top government officials, scholars, business executives, journalists, lawyers, and nonprofit professionals. Membership is composed of those residing in the greater New York and Washington, DC, areas, with a plurality based around the United States and abroad.

CFR members enjoy unparalleled access to a nonpartisan forum through which they engage with and gain insight from experts in international affairs. Members have in-person access to world leaders, senior government officials, members of Congress, and prominent thinkers and practitioners in academia, policy, and business, many of whom are members themselves. Convening nearly one thousand events annually, CFR is dedicated to facilitating an intellectual exchange of ideas through expert panel discussions, symposia, town halls, livestreams, and CEO forums exclusively for members. Through exposure to CFR's think tank, publications, briefing materials, and special content on CFR.org and ForeignAffairs.com, members benefit from an expansive collection of unmatched intellectual capital and resources.

The Council seeks quality, diversity, and balance in its membership. Criteria for membership include intellectual achievement and expertise; degree of experience, interest, and current involvement in international affairs; promise of future achievement and service in foreign relations; potential contributions to CFR's work; desire and ability to participate in CFR activities; and standing among peers. New members are elected twice a year by the Board of Directors.

Applying for Membership

Eligibility Requirements

- Membership is restricted to U.S. citizens (native born or naturalized) and permanent residents who have applied to become citizens. Permanent residents must email a statement to applications@cfr.org indicating their current citizenship and the date of their formal application for U.S. citizenship.

- CFR visiting fellows are prohibited from applying for membership until they have completed their fellowship tenure.

- CFR members are required to fulfill annual dues requirements.

Candidates must submit an online application, complete with a nominating letter from a current CFR member and seconding letters from three to four other individuals.

To apply for membership, visit cfr.org/membership/individual-membership.

Membership Deadlines and Candidate Notification

The two annual membership application deadlines are March 1 and November 1. All membership candidates and their letter writers will receive notification of the election decisions in late June for the March 1 deadline, and in mid-March for the November 1 deadline.

Stephen M. Kellen
Term Member Program

The Stephen M. Kellen Term Member Program, established in 1970 to cultivate the next generation of foreign policy leaders, encourages professionals from diverse backgrounds to engage in a sustained conversation on international affairs and U.S. foreign policy. Each year, a new class of term members between the ages of thirty and thirty-six is elected to serve a fixed five-year term. Term members enjoy a full range of activities, including events with high-profile speakers; an annual Term Member Conference; roundtables; trips to various sites, including military bases, international organizations, and U.S. governmental agencies; and one weeklong study trip abroad every two years.

For more information on the Term Member Program, please visit cfr.org/membership/term-member-program.

Applying for Term Membership
Eligibility Requirements

- Term membership is restricted to U.S. citizens (native born or naturalized) and permanent residents who have applied to become citizens. Permanent residents must email a statement to applications@cfr.org indicating their current citizenship and the date of their formal application for U.S. citizenship.

- Candidates for term membership must be between the ages of thirty and thirty-six on January 1 of the year in which they apply.

- CFR visiting fellows are prohibited from applying for term membership until they have completed their fellowship tenure.

- Graduate students should generally wait until after the completion of their degree to apply for term membership.

- CFR term members are required to fulfill annual dues requirements.

Term membership candidates must submit an online application, complete with a nominating letter from a current CFR member and seconding letters from two to three other individuals.

To apply for term membership, visit cfr.org/membership/individual-membership.

Term Membership Deadline and Candidate Notification

The annual application deadline for term membership is January 3. All term membership candidates and their letter writers will receive notification of the election decisions in late June.

To learn more about the membership application process or for information on nominating a candidate, visit cfr.org/membership or contact Nancy D. Bodurtha, vice president, meetings and membership, at 212.434.9456 or applications@cfr.org.

Profile of the Membership

Between July 2018 and June 2019, CFR membership decreased by 0.08 percent, from 5,103 to 5,099 members.

Member records are maintained by CFR at 58 East 68th Street, New York, NY 10065.

Location	Number of Members	Percentage of Membership
National	2,000	39
New York Area	1,600	32
Washington, DC, Area	1,499	29
Total	5,099	100

Industry	Number of Members	Percentage of Membership
Education	1,090	22
Nonprofit and International Organizations	1,028	20
Financial Institutions	773	15
Law and Consulting	685	13
Government	359	7
Media and News Services	317	6
Commerce	160	3
Information Technology	127	3
Military	100	2
Medicine and Health Care	46	1
Energy and Power	37	1
Other	377	7
Total	5,099	100

5,099
individual members

New York City Area
1,600

Washington, DC, Area
1,499

National
2,000

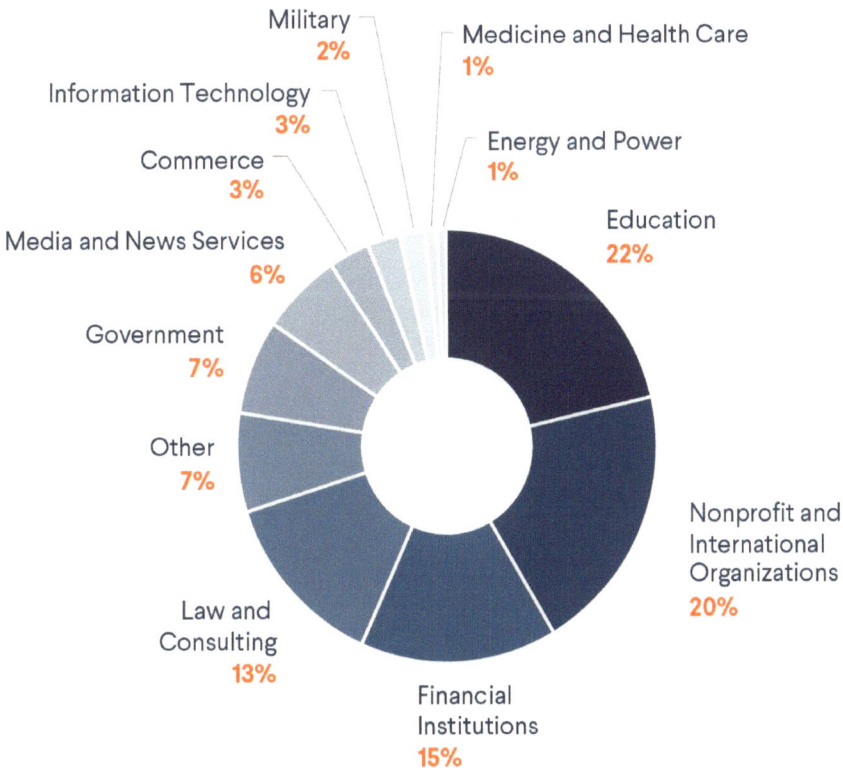

Military
2%

Medicine and Health Care
1%

Information Technology
3%

Energy and Power
1%

Commerce
3%

Media and News Services
6%

Education
22%

Government
7%

Other
7%

Nonprofit and International Organizations
20%

Law and Consulting
13%

Financial Institutions
15%

Corporate Program

Profile of the Corporate Program Membership

Founded in 1953 with twenty-five corporate members, the Corporate Program has since expanded to include nearly 140 companies from various industries and regions of the world. Through CFR's unmatched convening power, the program links private-sector leaders with decision-makers from government, media, nongovernmental organizations, and academia to discuss issues at the intersection of business and foreign policy.

Beginning in fiscal year 2020, corporate membership will be available at three levels: Founders ($100,000), President's Circle ($75,000), and Affiliates ($40,000). Member companies are offered briefings by in-house experts, a members-only website with CFR resources tailored to the private sector, and roundtables designed specifically for executives. The highlight of the program year is the annual Corporate Conference, which addresses such topics as competitiveness, geopolitical risk, and the global economic outlook. Additionally, the program provides professional development opportunities for individuals on a senior management track through its Corporate Leaders Program, and, for those with fewer than ten years of experience, through its Young Professionals Briefing series.

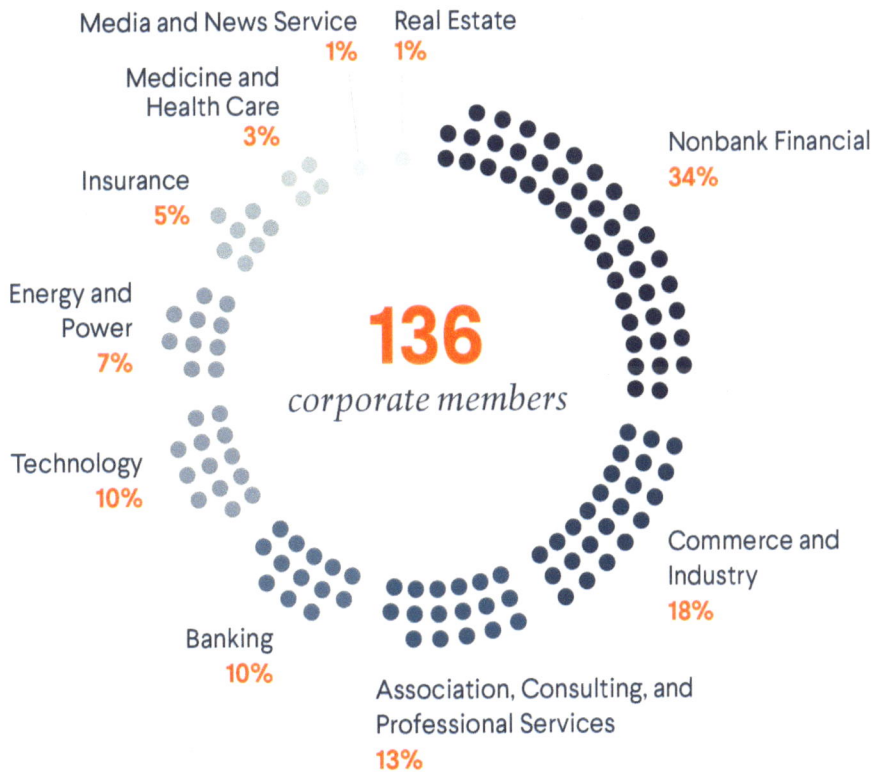

136 corporate members

- Media and News Service 1%
- Real Estate 1%
- Medicine and Health Care 3%
- Insurance 5%
- Energy and Power 7%
- Technology 10%
- Banking 10%
- Association, Consulting, and Professional Services 13%
- Association, Consulting, and Professional Services 13%
- Commerce and Industry 18%
- Nonbank Financial 34%

Note: Percentages do not total 100% due to rounding.

Benefits of Corporate Program Membership

Founders ($100,000+)

All President's Circle and Affiliates benefits plus:

- Four CFR fellow briefings tailored to the company's interests

- Professional development opportunity for four rising executives to participate as "Corporate Leaders" in conjunction with the competitive Stephen M. Kellen Term Member Program

- One rental of the historic Harold Pratt House ballroom and library (based on availability)

- Prominent logo placement on the Corporate Program webpage and at the Corporate Conference

- Online site license arrangements and fifteen *Foreign Affairs* print subscriptions

- One cover advertisement and sponsored content package in *Foreign Affairs*, both in print and online

President's Circle ($75,000, effective July 1, 2019)

All Affiliates benefits plus:

- Invitations for leadership-level executives to attend the Chairman's Circle Dinner and the Annual Dinner with CFR's Board of Directors and Global Board of Advisors

- Opportunities for senior executives to participate in study groups and roundtables led by CFR fellows, and attend exclusive events with noted thinkers and practitioners in government, policy, academia, and the private sector

- Priority registration for meetings, roundtables, and high-level events

- Two CFR fellow briefings tailored to the company's interests

- Professional development opportunity for two rising executives to participate as "Corporate Leaders" in conjunction with the competitive Stephen M. Kellen Term Member Program

- Ten *Foreign Affairs* print subscriptions

- One in-book page advertisement in *Foreign Affairs*, both in print and online

Affiliates ($40,000, effective July 1, 2019)

- Invitations for executives to attend a range of CFR events each year in New York, Washington, DC, and other major cities in the United States and around the world

- Opportunities for senior executives to participate in special meetings and round-tables with CFR's president

- Invitations for executives to attend the Corporate Conference, CFR's annual summit on geopolitical and geoeconomic issues of interest to the global business community

- One CFR fellow briefing tailored to the company's interests

- Participation in rapid-response conference calls by CFR fellows and other experts

- Opportunities for young professionals to participate in special briefings, select meetings, and conference calls

- Access to meeting replays, conference calls, and other digital resources, including the member services portal

- Six *Foreign Affairs* print subscriptions

- Exclusive corporate rates on additional *Foreign Affairs* subscriptions, advertising, and custom events with editors

- Reduced rates for rental of the Harold Pratt House in New York City and 1777 F Street in Washington, DC

- Recognition on CFR's corporate membership roster

Note: *Corporate membership dues are 65 percent tax deductible.*
For more information, please contact the Corporate Program at corporate@cfr.org or 212.434.9684.

Financial Highlights

Statement of Financial Position

As of June 30, 2019 (with comparative totals for June 30, 2018)

Assets	2019	2018
Cash and cash equivalents	$ 33,648,800	$ 25,995,200
Accounts receivable, net	3,178,000	2,107,500
Prepaid expenses	1,040,400	1,001,900
Grants and contributions receivable, net	23,569,900	26,363,900
Contributions receivable for endowment, net	20,136,100	22,495,500
Inventory	52,700	65,500
Investments	475,831,800	448,130,400
Land, buildings and building improvements, and equipment, net	68,866,000	71,086,300
Total assets	**626,323,700**	**597,246,200**

Liabilities		
Accounts payable and accrued expenses	8,515,200	7,983,400
Deferred revenue	6,523,400	6,078,300
Accrued postretirement benefits	5,852,000	5,248,000
Interest-rate swap agreement	6,912,200	3,858,900
Bonds payable	52,493,200	54,520,000
Total liabilities	**80,296,000**	**77,688,600**

Net assets		
Without donor restrictions	116,990,300	101,475,600
With donor restrictions	429,037,400	418,082,000
Total net assets	**546,027,700**	**519,557,600**
Total liabilities and net assets	**$626,323,700**	**$597,246,200**

Note: To view the full 2019 Financial Statements, please visit cfr.org/annual-report-2019.

Statement of Activities

For the year ended June 30, 2019

Operating revenue and support	Without donor restrictions	With donor restrictions	Total
Membership dues	$ 7,337,600	$ —	$ 7,337,600
Annual giving	10,497,000	—	10,497,000
Corporate memberships and related income	5,934,700	172,700	6,107,400
Grants and contributions	2,065,100	22,960,500	25,025,600
Foreign Affairs publications	9,238,200	—	9,238,200
Investment return used for current operations	5,512,600	15,072,100	20,584,700
Rental income	1,967,100	—	1,967,100
Miscellaneous	952,200	—	952,200
Net assets released from restrictions	32,481,200	(32,481,200)	—
Total operating revenue and support	**75,985,700**	**5,724,100**	**81,709,800**

Operating expenses

Program expenses:			
Studies Program	23,551,800	—	23,551,800
Task Force	297,600	—	297,600
NY Meetings	1,378,500	—	1,378,500
DC programs	1,881,300	—	1,881,300
Special events	1,217,100	—	1,217,100
Foreign Affairs	10,417,800	—	10,417,800
National Program	1,429,400	—	1,429,400
Outreach Program	2,016,500	—	2,016,500
Term member	526,600	—	526,600
Digital Program	5,638,100	—	5,638,100
Education Program	3,752,300	—	3,752,300
Global Board of Advisors	102,300	—	102,300
Total program expenses	**$52,209,300**	**$ —**	**$52,209,300**

Note: To view the full 2019 Financial Statements, please visit cfr.org/annual-report-2019.

	Without donor restrictions	With donor restrictions	Total
Supporting services:			
Fundraising:			
Development	$ 2,454,900	$ —	$ 2,454,900
Corporate Program	2,166,500	—	2,166,500
Total fundraising	**4,621,400**	**–**	**4,621,400**
Management and general	17,040,900	—	17,040,900
Membership	1,792,500	—	1,792,500
Total supporting services	**23,454,800**	**–**	**23,454,800**
Total operating expenses	**75,664,100**	**–**	**75,664,100**
Excess of operating revenue and support over operating expenses	**321,600**	**5,724,100**	**6,045,700**
Nonoperating activities			
Investment loss in excess of spending rate	(2,357,400)	(5,821,700)	(8,179,100)
Endowment contributions	20,650,000	11,606,800	32,256,800
Change in value of interest-rate swap agreement	(3,053,300)	—	(3,053,300)
Other	553,800	(553,800)	—
Total nonoperating activities	**15,793,100**	**5,231,300**	**21,024,400**
Changes in net assets before postretirement changes other than net periodic costs	16,114,700	10,955,400	27,070,100
Postretirement changes other than net periodic costs	(600,000)	—	(600,000)
Change in net assets	**15,514,700**	**10,955,400**	**26,470,100**
Net assets, beginning of year	**101,475,600**	**418,082,000**	**519,557,600**
Net assets, end of year	**$116,990,300**	**$429,037,400**	**$546,027,700**

Statement of Activities

For the year ended June 30, 2018

Operating revenue and support	Without donor restrictions	With donor restrictions	Total
Membership dues	$ 6,960,000	$ —	$ 6,960,000
Annual giving	10,600,500	—	10,600,500
Corporate memberships and related income	5,194,500	197,000	5,391,500
Grants and contributions	1,527,300	29,999,400	31,526,700
Foreign Affairs publications	9,489,800	—	9,489,800
Investment return used for current operations	5,336,900	14,078,200	19,415,100
Rental income	1,979,100	—	1,979,100
Miscellaneous	489,700	—	489,700
Net assets released from restrictions	31,469,600	(31,469,600)	—
Total operating revenue and support	**73,047,400**	**12,805,000**	**85,852,400**

Operating expenses

Program expenses:			
Studies Program	24,434,900	—	24,434,900
Task Force	425,900	—	425,900
NY Meetings	1,557,400	—	1,557,400
DC programs	1,728,400	—	1,728,400
Special events	1,154,300	—	1,154,300
Foreign Affairs	10,354,600	—	10,354,600
National Program	1,351,400	—	1,351,400
Outreach Program	1,974,400	—	1,974,400
Term member	366,500	—	366,500
Digital Program	5,389,900	—	5,389,900
Education Program	2,450,000	—	2,450,000
Global Board of Advisors	86,700	—	86,700
Total program expenses	**$51,274,400**	**$ —**	**$51,274,400**

Note: To view the full 2019 Financial Statements, please visit cfr.org/annual-report-2019.

	Without donor restrictions	With donor restrictions	Total
Supporting services:			
Fundraising:			
Development	$ 2,542,000	$ —	$ 2,542,000
Corporate Program	1,764,100	—	1,764,100
Total fundraising	**4,306,100**	**–**	**4,306,100**
Management and general	15,403,600	—	15,403,600
Membership	1,688,000	—	1,688,000
Total supporting services	**21,397,700**	**–**	**21,397,700**
Total operating expenses	**72,672,100**	**–**	**72,672,100**
Excess of operating revenue and support over operating expenses	**375,300**	**12,805,000**	**13,180,300**
Nonoperating activities			
Investment gain in excess of spending rate	409,600	9,305,800	9,715,400
Endowment contributions	—	12,285,400	12,285,400
Change in value of interest-rate swap agreement	2,258,500	—	2,258,500
Other	954,000	—	954,000
Reclassification of gift proceeds due to clarified donor intent	24,847,700	(24,847,700)	—
Total nonoperating activities	**28,469,800**	**(3,256,500)**	**25,213,300**
Changes in net assets before postretirement changes other than net periodic costs	28,845,100	9,548,500	38,393,600
Postretirement changes other than net periodic costs	646,000	—	646,000
Change in net assets	**29,491,100**	**9,548,500**	**39,039,600**
Net assets, beginning of year	**71,984,500**	**408,533,500**	**480,518,000**
Net assets, end of year	**$101,475,600**	**$418,082,000**	**$519,557,600**

Credits

Editor: Patricia Dorff
Production Editor: Julie Hersh
Associate Editor: Chloe Moffett
Staff Editor: Sumit Poudyal
Photo Editor: Hunter Hallman
Copy Editor: Glenn Court
Cover Design: Sabine Baumgartner and
Cayla Merrill
Production: Gene Crofts
Publications Intern: Caroline Fernandez

Photos

Don Pollard: 11 top, bottom; 15 top left, top
right; 16 left; 17; 24 left

Kaveh Sardari/www.sardari.com:
15 bottom; 21 bottom; 22; 27 bottom; 30

Eli Pitta: 16 right

Melanie Einzig: 19; 21 top

East Asia Institute: 23

Jim Bowen and Greg Kubik/The Texas Crew:
24 right

Veronica Bernie: 27 top

Siphiwe Sibeko/Reuters: 29 top

*Note: All titles and affiliations referenced in the
Annual Report, including captions, were current
at the time of the event.*

www.ingramcontent.com/pod-product-compliance
Lightning Source LLC
Chambersburg PA
CBHW060829270326
41931CB00003B/108

9 780876 097786